## Parallel Li

**Katherine Chandler** is a Welsh pla~~~ ~~ ~~~~~~ ~~~~ ~~~
been produced by companies such as National Theatre
Wales, Bristol Old Vic, Sherman Cymru, Pentabus Theatre,
Theatr Nan'Og and Dirty Protest. She was the inaugural
Winner of the BBC and National Theatre Wales, Wales
Drama Award, with *Parallel Lines*. Her first play, *Before it
Rains*, won the Writers' Guild Playwright award, Theatre
Critics of Wales award, and was a finalist for the Susan
Smith Blackburn prize. Her play *Bird* won the 2013
Bruntwood Judges'prize. Her adaptation of Terry Jones's
fairytales *The Silly Kings* was produced by National Theatre
Wales in Cardiff Castle, and her play *Hood* was performed as
part of the National Theatre Connections.

Katherine Chandler

# Parallel Lines

Bloomsbury Methuen Drama
An imprint of Bloomsbury Publishing Plc

# BLOOMSBURY

LONDON • OXFORD • NEW YORK • NEW DELHI • SYDNEY

**Bloomsbury Methuen Drama**
An imprint of Bloomsbury Publishing Plc

| | |
|---|---|
| 50 Bedford Square | 1385 Broadway |
| London | New York |
| WC1B 3DP | NY 10018 |
| UK | USA |

www.bloomsbury.com

**Bloomsbury is a registered trademarks of Bloomsbury Publishing Plc**

First published in 2015 by Methuen Drama in *Contemporary Welsh Plays*
Published in this edition in 2015

**British Library Cataloguing-in-Publication Data**
A catalogue record for this book is available from the British Library.

ISBN: PB: 978-1-4742-6000-8
ePub: 978-1-4742-6002-2
ePDF: 978-1-4742-6001-5

**Library of Congress Cataloging-in-Publication Data**
A catalog record for this book is available from the Library of Congress.

Typeset by Country Setting, Kingsdown, Kent CT14 8ES
Printed and bound in Great Britain

# Parallel Lines

For Guy

## Acknowledgements

Simon Nehan, Siwan Morris, Amy Ffion Edwards,
Nia Gwynne, John Mcgrath and Kate Rowlands.

*Parallel Lines* received its world premiere on 20 November 2013 at Chapter Arts Centre, Cardiff, and won the inaugural Wales Drama Award. The production featured the following cast:

| | |
|---|---|
| **Steph** | Rachel Redford |
| **Melissa** | Jan Anderson |
| **Julia** | Lisa Diveney |
| **Simon** | Gareth Pierce |

| | |
|---|---|
| *Director* | Catherine Paskell |
| *Designer* | Signe Beckmann |
| *Lighting Designer* | Jason Osterman |
| *Sound Designer* | Dan Lawrence |
| *Fight Director* | Kev McCurdy |
| *Assistant Director* | Anna Poole |

'If anyone injures his neighbour, whatever he has done must be done to him: fracture for fracture, eye for eye, tooth for tooth. As he has injured the other, so he is to be injured.'

Leviticus, Old Testament

## Notes

*Parallel lines: Two lines that are parallel never meet, never cross over one another. This should be reflected in the staging of the two worlds within the play.*

*There is a feeling of symmetry in the play. Both women are thiry-five, both families are affected by the events.*

*Melissa and Steph's relationship is fiery and physical and immediate. Zero to a hundred and back again in a matter of seconds.*

*Movement and physicality is important for this play in order to express the symmetry of the piece and the emotion and narrative of the scenes, where there is no dialogue.*

*denotes when action should be simultaneous.

*A sparse kitchen. Morning.*

*Steph, fifteen, looks through the cupboards for something to eat. Pulls out a bowl for cereal. Gives it a wipe with her t-shirt. Picks at something stuck in the bowl. Grabs a lonely packet of supermarket own brand sugary cereal. The dregs of the packet spill out. She hunts for milk. None in the fridge. Looks at the kitchen table at a carton of milk that's been sitting there overnight. She sniffs it. Stinks. Dips her finger in the dregs of a sugar packet. Sucks her finger. Looks around for something else to eat. There's nothing. Starts to eat the dry cereal leaning against the units.*

*Melissa thiry-five, with a banging hangover enters.*

*Repeats the same actions as her daughter. Looks through the cupboards for something to eat. Grabs the same lonely packet of supermarket own brand sugary cereal looks inside. Empty...*

**Steph**   There's nothing.

**Melissa**   What you eating then?

**Steph**   Nothing.

*Melissa flicks the switch on the kettle. Grabs a packet of fags from the side. Lights it. Looks for the milk.*

*Sniffs the milk. Recoils. Pauses. Bites the bullet.*

**Melissa**   Go down the shop for me, Steph.

**Steph**   No.

**Melissa**   Get us some milk. Some bread.

*Reaches for her handbag on the table, takes out her purse. No luck.*

**Steph**   No.

*Goes back to the bag. Empties it out. A fiver wrapped in a receipt.*

**Melissa**    Get yourself some sweets.

**Steph**    For fucks sake.

**Melissa**    Fags then. Cider, crack cocaine.

*Nothing. Exchange a glare.*

**Steph**    Shut up.

**Melissa**    Get some clothes on and get your arse down the shop.

*A look.*

You're going back, Monday. They said.

**Steph**    Is that what they said, is it.

*Melissa puts out two cups, adds two tea bags. Steph notices.*
*Melissa looks at her. Drags on her fag.*

**Melissa**    I got a letter. From school. They're on my case Steph. It
says you gotta go back.

**Steph**    I ain't going back.

**Melissa**    Monday.
They wants you in Monday morning. See how you goes.

**Steph**    See how I goes?

**Melissa**    You can't just sit on your arse, day in day out.

**Steph**    Like you.

*Drags her fag.*

**Melissa**    You needs to get out.

**Steph**    I likes to sit on my arse.

**Melissa**    Needs to put it behind you.

**Steph**    I likes it in.

**Melissa**    You've had long enough.

**Steph**    On my own. It's what I'm used to, ain't it.

**Melissa**    I was talking to Stacey Lee's Mam in the Lion last night. She works for social services don't she. She says you have to go back. It's the law. Says they'll be getting on me for keeping you off.

**Steph**    Stacey Lee's Mam knows shit all.

**Melissa**    Yeah well.

*Eyes up Steph.*

*Drags her fag.*

She's pregnant again, Steph. forty-four, she is. To a man called Hilary. Can you imagine.
A fucking man. Hilary. Why, for fucks sake. Janine reckons he's only twenty-seven?

**Steph**    I'm not going back.

**Melissa**    It was one of them nights, you know Steph. My sides cramped right up with laughing. Hilary, though.
'I'm a community van driver, in the community' he had one of them little high pitched voice like that. 'I got my own van'.
Sounds like that one of the Muppet show. What was his name. You know, that doctor one with the ginger hair.
And the nose. What's he called?

**Steph**    You said you wasn't going out. Last night.

**Melissa**    We watches them leave cos we can see the car park from the window and we're thinking where's this van then.
Janine's thinking it's one of them Beetles campers things. The only thing we can see Steph, is a sprayed ambulance you know one of them old ones they sell off. I didn't even notice it cos I'm thinking it's a wreck that's been left there. Anyway they only gets in this ambulance don't they. Laugh. Janine's pissed herself. She's grabbing herself and saying it's all down my leg and that's before we even seen the side of the van, you'll love this Steph, on the side he's painted 'give the old a sporting chance'. And she's sat there smiling at us out of the window.
What a night.

*Melissa grabs an near empty pack of sugar and sucks her finger then dips it into the packet. She eats the sugar.*

**Melissa**   I'm paying for it now though. Jesus.

*Melissa rubs her head.*

**Melissa**   Go down the shop Steph, my head's banging.

**Steph**   No.

**Melissa**   You're going back.

**Steph**   Am I.

*Pours water in the cups.*

**Melissa**   Get some exams. Get a good job.

**Steph**   Don't give me all that. Don't give me all that, like you gives a shit about me getting a good job an that. You wants me back in school so they don't come round yer again. So they don't start giving you any shit.
You're so full of it.
So fucking transparent.

**Melissa**   Transparent. Transparent am I. You didn't learn words like that from me. I gave you the shit and the fuck but transparent. Well. Now we knows. You're definitely going back, you.
Learn yourself some more of them words.

**Steph**   You don't care about what I learns.

**Melissa**   No.

**Steph**   You don't care about nothing except when it affects you.

**Melissa**   Stop banging on Steph. Like a broken record. I don't want no one coming yer.

**Steph**   And finally the truth.

**Melissa**   Don't want them yer telling us how to be. Looking down their noses at us.
It'll be all that twitching and sniffing and looking like they don't wanna sit down in case they catches something.

It'll be all forms and whispers and briefcases. I'm not having that, Steph.

**Steph**   I'll leave. Go to a different school.

**Melissa**   D'you think I got the money to be putting you on a bus every day, getting you new uniform an all that.

**Steph**   Will he be there?

**Melissa**   I don't know. What if he is?

**Steph**   I don't wanna see him.

**Melissa**   You got nothing to hide. You got nothing to be ashamed of.
Him. That Simon. He's the one.
They should've pressed charges. But they looks after their own, that lot. That headmaster.
And in his eyes you ain't worth the paperwork. They should've gone to the police when they found that diary. Straight away. That's what they should've done.
Straight to the police.

**Steph**   Oh yeah? You wouldn't go to the police.

**Melissa**   *They* Steph, when it all came out, they should've done something.
I would though. I would, if it's what you wanted.

**Steph**   Let's go to the police.

**Melissa**   If that's what you want, that's fine with me. Is that what you want?
Cos I would, you know … I dunno, the police an that though Steph. They said didn't they, the school, they said they sorted it, didn't they?
They said it was nothing.

**Steph**   It weren't *nothing*.

**Melissa**   I know that … we know, don't we.
What happened.
The police mind.

We could Steph but, you know.
That's a right can of worms that is.

**Steph**   He'll be there. Simon. On Monday.

**Melissa**   I'll tell the head.
I'll say she don't want no contact. I'll say there'll be no contact at
all.

**Steph**   I'm not sitting there with the head. Talking about it all.

**Melissa**   I'll say that.
I'll say she's not coming in yer, talking about nothing.
Anyway, his room stinks.

**Steph**   He stinks.

**Melissa**   He fucking hums, Steph.
Shall I say that to him Steph, shall I? I'll say she ain't coming in
here cos you fucking hum, mate.
I could say that Steph, cos he wouldn't dare say nothing back, in
the circumstances like.

*Melissa laughs then spoons the tea bags out of the two cups and
chucks them into the sink.*

**Steph**   You weren't going out. That's what you said.

**Melissa**   It'll be good to see your friends though, won't it?

**Steph**   You said you'd stay with me.

**Melissa**   Good to be back in a routine.

**Steph**   Said we'd watch the telly.

**Melissa**   You gotta stop this Steph. You can't stay in forever.

**Steph**   I watched this thing about the soldiers from Iraq.

**Melissa**   You watched about Iraq?

*Melissa grabs an near empty pack of sugar and sucks her finger
then dips it into the packet. She eats the sugar.*

**Steph**   When you was out.

**Melissa**   What are you watching stuff about Iraq for?

**Steph**   About the soldiers when they come home it was. Got post-traumatic stress and all that.

**Melissa**   There's other stuff on – good stuff.

**Steph**   They went to this hospital but it weren't a hospital, you know, they were just all there …

**Melissa**   You should've seen Janine's dress.

**Steph**   … This big old house in the country.

**Melissa**   You'd have loved it, you would. Like an emerald green.

**Steph**   Some of them were just lying there like they was in cots.

**Melissa**   Green it was.

**Steph**   Cos the beds had bars.

**Melissa**   She's dark in' she.

**Steph**   Rails like if they was going to fall out.

**Melissa**   She can take all them lovely colours.

**Steph**   They was lying there and looking through the rails and I was thinking that it looked like they was in prison.

**Melissa**   Oh, happy days.

**Steph**   I thought to myself that they was.

**Melissa**   Can't you watch something normal.

**Steph**   I watched it. You was out.

**Melissa**   Christ d'you blame me? Watching that shit.

**Steph**   They're gonna close it. The hospital.

**Melissa**   Good.

**Steph**   Where did she go?

**Melissa**   Who?

**Steph**   Where did Janine go?

**Melissa**   Janine? What about Janine?

**Steph**   Where did she go?

**Melissa**   What you talking about?

**Steph**   Last night.
I'm talking about last night.

**Melissa**   What about last night?

**Steph**   Where did Janine go?

**Melissa**   I don't know. Home I s'pose.
Ain't that where people go.
After a night out.

**Steph**   He didn't go home.

**Melissa**   Who?

**Steph**   Him in your bed.

**Melissa**   Look at each other for as long as can get away with.

**Steph**   Probably haven't got a home.
Some pisshead looked at you longer than five seconds was it.

**Melissa**   He did go home.
My home.
My bed.

**Steph**   You said you wouldn't do that.

**Melissa**   Shut it, will you.

**Steph**   You said that wasn't gonna happen no more.

**Melissa**   Says a lot of things, don't I.

**Steph**   You said, Mam.

**Melissa**   Don't start *(wants to shout but aware of bloke upstairs)*.
Fucking going on. Just keep it down.

**Steph**   You said it would be different.

**Melissa**    Just fucking shut it.

*Silence.*

**Melissa**    Anyway you'd like him.
He was in Iraq.

**Steph**    He deserves better than you then.

**Melissa**    You're going to the shop.
And then you're going to make yourself scarce.
So you can stay in your room or better still get out.

**Steph**    I'm not going back.

**Melissa**    You're going back on Monday. And that's the last I
wants to hear about it.

**Steph**    Mam. Please.

**Melissa**    You're going back.

**Steph**    I can't Mam.

**Melissa**    You starts back Monday.

*Steph launches at her Mam, screams at her with such ferocity that
Melissa feels attacked.*

*After a while.*

**Melissa**    What is wrong with you.

*Beat.*

**Melissa**    Jesus Christ.

*Beat.*

**Melissa**    Get your arse down the shop.

*Melissa pulls leggings out of a laundry pile and chucks them and
the fiver at Steph.*

*Steph picks up the fiver.*

*Looks at her mother.*

*Leaves.*

**Melissa** *shocked in the kitchen.*

*\*Puts her head in her hands.*

*Takes a minute.*

*Gathers herself.*

*Picks up the two cups and heads with them back to the bedroom.*

*\*Julia thirty-five, enters her modern mod cons kitchen.*

*Makes a cup of fruit tea.*

*Takes her bag.*

*Takes out a make-up bag and checks her face.*

*Touches up her makeup.*

*Fusses around the kitchen, morning routine.*

*Simon thirty-five, enters.*

*Drying his hair with a towel.*

*Casual, t-shirt, jeans.*

**Simon**    Bloody shower.

**Julia**    Oh god. Not again.

**Simon**    We'll have to get it resealed because it's every time now.

**Julia**    Not every time.

**Simon**    I could do it?

**Julia**    If you like.

**Simon**    I think it's bowing, the ceiling.

**Julia**    It's not bowing.

**Simon**    Well, there's a patch. There's definitely a patch.

**Julia**    You need a hobby.

**Simon**   And it's right above where I sit. I keep thinking one day the whole bloody roof will cave in on me. And I'll be sat there in a mound of dust and plaster and floorboards and ceiling stuff.

**Julia**   That won't happen.

**Simon**   Or the water will get into the electrics and god, then what.
You'll have to go to B&Q and get something.

**Julia**   You really do need a hobby.

*Julia sips her herbal tea. Grimaces slightly.*

**Simon**   Coffee?

*Julia looks at her cup. Sniffs it. Recoils.*

**Julia**   I should give it a chance.

*Simon starts to make coffee.*

**Simon**   Never drink anything that you have to hang in your cup. It always tastes like shit.

**Julia**   Yeah, well.

**Simon**   What do you want for dinner?

**Julia**   Dinner?

**Julia**   It's twenty to eight in the morning. I don't know what I want for my dinner. I can just about stomach this ... (pause) Pasta's fine. It's fine.

**Simon**   I was thinking of pasta. But then I thought with that carb diet you go on? Are you on it today? I could do salmon? I'll go shopping ...

**Simon**   I'll make a pudding.

**Julia**   Not after pasta.

**Simon**   I'll make crumble?

**Julia**   I won't want it.

**Simon**    I'll get some wine?

**Julia**    I've got book club tomorrow.
I need a clear head, because I've not even started the book yet.
I've read the cover. Talking of which I need to bloody well find it
now. I'm sure I put it down on the table.

**Simon**    I've not seen it.

*Looks at her watch, takes a gulp of her tea, grimaces.*

**Julia**    Fucking 10S.

**Simon**    Fucking 10S.

**Julia**    Fucking Tyler Banks.

**Simon**    Fucking Tyler Banks.

**Julia**    He's an idiot and it's not like I haven't tried.

**Simon**    No.

**Julia**    I just want to kick his head in. Actually kick his head in.

**Simon**    I'll kick his head in. I'll follow him home.

**Julia**    I don't think …

**Simon**    I was joking.

*Pause.*

**Julia**    Pity.

**Simon**    In eight hours you'll be home.

**Julia**    I've got that thing.
That poetry slam. After school.

**Simon**    In nine hours you'll be home.

**Julia**    Yes.

**Simon**    And you can sit down and eat pasta and pretend to read
the book.
I'll print you off some reviews from Amazon so you can talk
about it tomorrow.

**Julia**    You'd do that for me.

**Simon**    I would, yes.

**Julia**    What are you doing today?

**Simon**    I thought I might go to the gym.

**Julia**    Right.

**Simon**    There are lots of old people at the gym I noticed. They have good trainers. Their clothes are ironed. When I say old I'm thinking over sixty-five.

**Julia**    Grey days they call them. You've gone on a grey day.

**Simon**    There's a difference that isn't obvious.
Not wrinkles and grey and obvious physicalities. Ironed tracksuits and brushed hair.

**Julia**    Ironed tracksuits!

**Simon**    It's true.
Signs that they're from a different time.

**Julia**    Okay.

**Simon**    There's this old guy. He's there all the time. He changes his shoes. So. He comes to the gym in his tracksuit and his shoes. Then he sits and he puts on his trainers. He works out a bit. Then he sits and puts his shoes back on.

**Julia**    With his ironed tracksuit.

**Simon**    Yes.
And I'm thinking. Just leave the trainers on. Don't worry about the trainers.

**Julia**    You definitely need a hobby.

**Simon**    But he's from an age that don't wear trainers.

**Julia**    That iron their tracksuits and brush their hair.

**Simon**    I don't think it's like that anymore. There aren't those clues.

**Julia**    You say that because you're thirty-five.

**Simon**    I say that because I noticed it.

**Julia**    You think you're twenty.

**Simon**    I notice things. I have time to notice things. Things I never noticed before. Like nature.

**Julia**    Nature?

**Simon**    I've started to notice nature.

**Julia**    You'll be ironing your tracksuit, soon.

**Simon**    I like its patience. It doesn't rush. In a world that's in a rush.
Nature happens when it's ready. In it's own time. I was thinking this because last year April was warm. When I was off? Do you remember?
And the April before that was warm. And so everyone thought 'Oh here we go, this is it, global warming'. And then we had the coldest June in the entire history of June. Do you remember? Last year.

**Julia**    I do, yes.

**Simon**    But the poppies were out in April.

**Julia**    I remember.

**Simon**    I remember thinking they were magnificent. That's not a word to use lightly but they were.
For a short time.
They were magnificent.

**Julia**    They were.

**Simon**    How things can change in a year because now it's June and the poppies are only just budding. They've thought 'April's a bit shit this year, we'll sit it out.'
And that's what they've done.

**Julia**    God, they're not dead are they.

**Simon**  They'll come when they're ready.

**Julia**  Yes.
And they'll be magnificent.

**Simon**  They want me in for two days.

**Julia**  What?

**Simon**  A phased return. They like to get you back. Quickly.

**Julia**  They want you in?

**Simon**  They want it all dealt with.
It's within a month. They want you back and. Everything back to normal. So.

**Julia**  When? What did he say?

**Simon**  He phoned me. Yesterday.

**Julia**  You didn't say.
He phoned you yesterday?

**Simon**  Yes. Two days a week he said. To start.

**Julia**  This week?

**Simon**  Next

**Julia**  Two days. For now.

**Simon**  Then within the month.

**Julia**  Back full time?

**Simon**  Yes.

**Julia**  Back to normal within the month.

**Simon**  That's how they do it.
When it's unsubstantiated so.
Everything forgotten.
Getting back to normal.

**Julia**  Back to normal.

**Simon**  I said, didn't I? I said it would be fine.

**Julia**    You did, yes.

**Simon**    I'm ready. I feel ready.

**Julia**    Will she be there?

**Simon**    Please Julia.

**Julia**    No. I know but it's –, but it just seems.
A month and then it's all done.

**Simon**    It's how they do it. To the letter he said.
Everything done – followed the book, so to speak.

**Julia**    That's great. It's great. It is. It's great.
It just seems quick but if that's how they do it.

**Simon**    That's how they do it.

**Julia**    Simon.

**Simon**    It feels like it's a start. Don't you think?

**Julia**    Simon …

**Simon**    I feel like we've turned a corner.

**Julia**    I can't find my book.

**Simon**    It'll turn up. And if it doesn't I'll buy you a new one.
We'll go into town and I'll treat you. We'll have dinner and
something fizzy.

**Julia**    Things are moving.

**Simon**    Yes. They are. We're moving on.

**Julia**    No.
Not that. Not you.

*Pause.*

Looks at Simon.

Starts packing her bag ready for work.

**Julia**    It doesn't matter.

*Julia looks at her watch.*

**Julia**   I should go.

*Pauses.*

**Julia**   I hope something happened to him on the way home from school last night. A hit and run. On a life support. I hope he's ill. Hope he's got something terminal.

**Simon**   He might have.

**Julia**   He won't see thirty. Possibly not even twenty.

**Simon**   Nine hours, that's all.

**Julia**   I had to tell him to stop looking at my arse the other day. I worried all day that I had spoken inappropriately to a minor. A minor to whom I had a duty of care …

**Simon**   Don't Julia.

**Julia**   … He's fifteen.
He thinks I would and he's fifteen …

**Simon**   Please don't.

**Julia**   … And I thought, can you imagine – both of us, God, that's all we need. After you?

*She looks at him. Moves past him to put her cup in the sink.*

*Starts to gather her things together for work.*

**Julia**   It makes you wonder why we do it?
Why anyone does it.
When some – little – on a whim – or for a laugh or –
There was a time, it was respected.
Being a teacher – I thought it was decent.
A respectful profession.

*Stops herself.*

*Takes a deep breath.*

**Julia**   I have to go.

*Puts last night's marking in a bag.*

*Exercise books.*

*Picks one up.*

*Flicks through it.*

*Looks at* **Simon**.

*Takes a moment.*

**Julia**   Nine hours and counting.

*Picks up her bags and leaves.*

*Simon takes a moment.*

*Looks around an empty kitchen.*

*\*Tidies a few things away.*

*Leaves the kitchen in his own time.*

*\*Melissa sits at table in darkness.*

*The sounds of late night radio in the background.*

*She sits smoking.*

*The light of the cigarette being dragged should be our only focus for a while.*

*We hear a key in a door and a door open and close. In darkness Steph enters the kitchen.*

**Melissa**   Alright, Steph?

**Steph**   For fuck's sake.
What the fuck are you doing sat there …

**Melissa**   You alright?

**Steph**   … Like a ghost.
A smoking ghost.
Or a nutter, like sat there, in the dark.

*Puts a lamp on.*

**Melissa**   Just sat here.

**Steph**   What's that?

*Goes to saucepan on the hob.*

**Steph**   Is that tea is it? Chilli?
What is that?
Is it that …

**Melissa**   It's Chilli.

**Steph**   Hot is it? Spicy?

**Melissa**   No.

**Steph**   I like it hot.

**Melissa**   Where've you been Steph?

**Steph**   Nicey, spicy.

**Melissa**   Where?

**Steph**   Out.

**Melissa**   Out.

**Steph**   Just out.

**Melissa**   It's one o'clock in the morning.

**Steph**   Time flies!

**Melissa**   I been worried.

**Steph**   Christ! Right. Sorry about that. It's just normally …

**Melissa**   I wondered where you was.

**Steph**   … you wouldn't give a shit.

**Melissa**   Night after night you're in. Like some sort of hermit.
And then tonight? Tonight you decides to go out?
Where?

**Steph**   Nowhere special.

**Melissa**   Where?

**Steph**    I fancied a walk.

**Melissa**    You been acting weird, Steph. Proper weird like. Since you been back in school.

**Steph**    I like walking. Getting my exercise. There's an obesity epidemic, haven't you heard.
I. Can't. Sleep.
So I walks.

*Pause.*

**Melissa**    In the dark?

**Steph**    Dark don't frighten me.

**Melissa**    You'll end up dead.
There'll be a knock on my door …

**Steph**    It feels like home.

**Melissa**    You're talking shit, Steph.

**Steph**    I like its truth.

**Melissa**    Its truth?

**Steph**    It don't pretend to be anything other than what it is.

**Melissa**    D'you think I'm a fucking idiot.

**Steph**    Lovely as it's been, chatting with you Mother – I'm going to bed.

**Melissa**    Do I look like a fucking idiot to you?

**Steph**    Yes.

*Melissa grabs at Steph looks for tracks on her arms. Her eyes. Melissa knows what to look for. Grabs Steph's bag roots through it. Empties it out onto the floor.*

**Steph**    For fuck's sake. I'm not you. I'm not you yet am I.

*She grabs her bag back. Scrambles her things back into it. As she puts things back in Melissa talks.*

**Melissa**   Got all your things …

**Steph**   I have, yes.

**Melissa** … got your purse …
and your keys there … and your keyring – got that when we was
in Devon. I knew you'd have that.
Headphones.
They'll be in there somewhere.
I know.
I knows what you got in there.
Could have told you without looking.
I. Know. You.

**Steph** *has finished putting her things back in the bag.*

**Steph**   I'm going to bed.

**Melissa**   You don't keep a diary, Steph.

**Steph**   You what?

**Melissa**   When they said diary? At first I was like. It was – shock
and then …
But it was all confused cos there was this Simon and he was your
teacher and they was saying about you being fifteen like and then
I didn't think. But then I thought.
They had this diary. Your diary. That's what they said.

**Steph**   That's right.

**Melissa**   And they said that no one knew nothing about it, all this
stuff with that teacher but then they found this diary and they had
to. They had to act on it. Any implication they said.

**Steph**   What are you saying?

**Melissa**   You never had a diary.

**Steph**   You saw it.
The head. He had it. It was on his desk.

**Melissa**   First time I seen it. How did it get there?

**Steph**    Someone found it. Gave it to him. Cos of what was in it.
You knows this.

**Melissa**    I thinks you've done something.
I don't know what.
But you have, I can see it in you.
You've done something and you ain't telling me.
And I needs to know. Because I can't do nothing to help you
unless I knows.

**Steph**    Help me?

**Melissa**    Yes.

**Steph**    You? Help me? Jesus.

**Melissa** *looks at* **Steph**.

**Steph**    Remember Davey, Mam.

**Melissa**    What? Davey?

**Steph**    You remember Davey. Course you do.

**Melissa**    What d'you think you're doing?

**Steph**    How old was I then?

**Melissa**    What are you bringing all that up for?

**Steph**    I was eleven.

**Melissa**    Shut up.

**Steph**    He was an animal.

**Melissa**    D'you think I don't know that?
Is that what you think?

**Steph**    I found him.
After he left us.
I looked for him.
He was with someone.

**Melissa**    I know what you're doing.

**Steph**    What was he called, that one that took us to
Alton Towers?
Ritchie was it?
Something like that.

**Melissa**    I know what you think you're doing.

**Steph**    Truth Melissa.
How old was I?

**Melissa**    You was six. Seven, you was seven.

**Steph**    I was eight.

**Melissa**    That's right.

**Steph**    He took us there for my birthday. To Alton Towers. He
left us there.

**Melissa**    I wants to know where you been.

**Steph**    I saw him. About a week after.
Walking up the high street pushing a pram with some kids.

**Melissa**    I don't want to know.

**Steph**    One was about four or something walking behind him,
struggling to keep up.

**Melissa**    I'm not listening to this.

**Steph**    Other one about eight.

**Melissa**    I want you to tell me where you been.

**Steph**    A girl. Like me. Eight. Looked like me. An she was
looking at him all adoring. Like me.

**Melissa**    Where have you been, Stephanie?

**Steph**    I told you, I been walking.

**Melissa**    I don't believe you.

**Steph**    I been to the canal. Stormy's. Even went down as far as
the viaduct Mam.
That's where I been.

An I'll go there again, if I wants.

**Melissa**    I won't have you there.

**Steph**    It's dark there.
You can't see the ground in front of you it's so dark. Pitch black it is.
There's this street lamp down the Ash path, it buzzes. I think it's the oldest street lamp ever. That lamp have seen some things, I bet Mam.
It looked like a star, so I followed it.
Just at the end of the path, in the shadows. This man's stood there. He looks like he's part of the shadows, it's so dark. I can't see his face.

**Melissa**    You don't go there. You hear me. I don't want you there.

**Steph**    He's got his cock in his hand. Just stood there with it in his hand. I stares at him.
And then I walks on.
Who I used to be.
She would have screamed.
But me, I just looks at him and he knows not to fuck with me and I walks past him and he was right. He was right not to fuck with me. I thought he was disappointed.
A disappointed man.
It's all in yer.
It's how you deal with it. I knows that now. I faced it.
I walks.
In the dark.
In the night. I goes wherever I wants.
People goes down Stormy's in their cars to fuck each other.
All sorts of people. All sorts of cars.
Police comes and everyone scarpers. They let them, the police, they don't do nothing.
Maybe it's truth, Mam. Maybe that's it.
You wants to talk about truth.
People wants to fuck each other, Isn't that the truth. In cars, in lanes, toilets, whatever, it's the truth of people.

The Via Duct is different though.
You knows about the Via Duct, Mam.

**Melissa**  *I don't.*
No, Steph. Don't say that. You don't say that.

**Steph**  Truth Melissa!
I think it's sad. A sad place.
Full of sad people with fucked up lives. And I thinks, how?
How did they get there? How did they get to this? What was it?
What happened that got them there? Cos you're not just born into
it, are you. You're not born into being fucked up?
Or is that it? Is that what it is, some of us – that's what we're
meant to be.

**Melissa**  You're not that. You're not. You're not that.

**Steph**  I went up the old railway line at the backs of them big
houses on Wordsworth court.
No one goes up there, not in the dark.
It started to rain so I sat under the trees and brambles and it was
like an umbrella.
Nature, it looks after you, don't it.
I liked sitting there in the dark and the rain. You can see in the
houses.
I goes in the gardens and they don't know I'm there.
I like it.
I likes watching them. People.
All doing the same things in different ways. Their houses all looks
the same, like hotels. Like they wears uniforms.
It's like they're showing off by not showing off nothing about
themselves.
But you know what Mam, when their doors are closed they're all
crying, shitting and fucking the same as the rest of us.
I went in to one of them.
The door was open and I went in.

**Melissa**  What did you do?

**Steph**  It was clean. Smelt like talc.

**Melissa**    What did you do, Steph?

**Steph**    I'm not afraid no more.
Not of nothing.
Not of the dark.
Not of the night.
Not of the shadows.
Nothing.

**Melissa**    Then God help you.

**Melissa** *leaves.*

**Steph**    He won't help me.

**Steph** *stands in the kitchen.*

*\*Breathing.*

*Breathing.*

*For a moment we see the child.*

*The music is on the radio.*

*She moves.*

*Dances.*

*Innocent.*

*The music slowly builds as she breathes.*

*She starts to really move to the music.*

*Dances.*

*Sexualized.*

*Abandoned.*

*Lights and music fades to darkness.*

*\*Simon is in a shirt and trousers. A loosened tie.*

*He's sat at table with a carrier bag open and papers of some sort strewn over the table.*

*He has a pencil in his mouth.*

*He's looking at the papers.*

*Puts down the pencil.*

*Rubs his brow.*

*Rubs his temples.*

*Head in hands.*

*Deep breathes.*

*Leans back in chair, head back, closes his eyes, breathes.*

*Breathes.*

*Back to it.*

*Picks up the pencil.*

*Looks at the papers.*

*Pushes the papers off the table on to the floor.*

*Frustrated with himself.*

*Holds the pencil in fists.*

*Pencil bends, bends ...*

*Snaps.*

*We hear the front door close and Julia sigh.*

*Simon sits up quickly hides pencil and picks up papers from floor.*

*Julia enters the kitchen with bags for life full of food.*

**Simon**    Bloody things. Had them piled and then once one goes, they all ...
I'll have to get another briefcase, replace that one I lost.

*Julia hasn't noticed. She gets straight into emptying bags into fridge and cupboards.*

**Julia**    Two birthdays and a new baby. Thirty quid. And the worst of it, is that the new baby is Sean Watts from the English

Dept. So Sue McGillis or should I say saint Sue says we should get a special something just from us because a new life is such a wonderful gift. I did this face (does face) and I was thinking if the new baby is such a wonderful gift then why am I forking out an extra twenty quid for another gift.

**Simon**    Did you say that?

**Julia**    I was thinking it.

**Simon**    It was always a fiver. That was the rule. Regardless of occasion.

**Julia**    Which is exactly what Jean Pritchard said. She said for a new baby she was only prepared to give a fiver. She's got four children and 16 grandchildren of her own to fork out for.

**Simon**    Fair comment.

*Stops for a second.*

**Julia**    How did it go?

**Simon**    Okay.

**Julia**    Okay?

**Simon**    Good. I don't know. Okay. It went.

**Julia**    Nothing happened?

**Simon**    No. It was fine.

**Julia**    No incidents?

**Simon**    Incident free. He said next week.

**Julia**    Full time?

**Simon**    Yes. Back to full time.

**Julia**    Right.
You're okay with that?

**Simon**    I am. Yes.
Yes, I think it'll be fine.

*Back to unpacking bags.*

**Simon**    He asked me to get his dry cleaning at lunchtime. I
wanted to tell him shove his job. I came this close. Of course
Seth Roberts saw me in the car park. His year eights have won
the under fourteens South West cup so he was 'up for the craic'
as they say. He sees that I'm carrying the Head's dry cleaning and
he hilariously takes to calling me 'Jeeves', for the rest of the day.
'Isn't that so, Jeeves,' 'What does Jeeves think about this'. I could
look at other jobs. I thought of gardening.

**Julia**    You're a teacher.

**Simon**    I thought of everything I put you through.

**Julia**    Head of department.

**Simon**    The way he looks at me. I wanted to walk out.

**Julia**    No talk of getting back into the classroom?

**Simon**    I'm still in the office. I've not yet been unleashed.
Although I've been given things to mark. I think it's a step up.

**Julia**    There's some soup in the fridge. Left over from yesterday.
I bought the bread you like.

**Simon**    Although I am good with systems and organisation so I
was a good filer, better than Ann Marie, I thought.
I walked from the office to the dinner hall. Third period.

**Julia**    A snack before this evening.

**Simon**    This evening?

**Julia**    We said we'd go. Max and Henry? We did say. Are you
sure today was okay?

**Simon**    It's come to my attention that a handful of the female
staff have made the decision to have no further contact with me.
Since my return I mean.
Which is entirely reprehensible all things considered.

**Julia**    Oh.

*Julia stops.*

*Her mood has changed.*

*We physically see the change in Julia throughout this speech.*

*She listens to him.*

**Simon**   I was in the Staff room, sat in my usual chair. Jennifer Hodge and her ridiculous tambourine and Grace Simons were sat opposite. I'd filled and turned on the kettle and was flicking through a holiday brochure one of the mid-day supes had left. Vanessa Harris came in and booms over 'Time for a Tetleys' and the others dutifully laugh even though I've heard it at least fifty times since I've been back and believe me it wasn't remotely funny the first time. So I lift my head and say, 'Milk no sugar thank you Vanessa'. I could visibly see them shuffle. They exchanged looks. So I think 'Let's let this one play itself out and see where they take it'. Vanessa is in the mug cupboard so I call over. 'Mines got a rose on,' I say. No response. She places four mugs next to the kettle. Jen's red and white polka dot, Gracey's floral china and Vanessa's piglet. Next to them is a Woolworth's general purpose, chipped and tannin stained, no sign of my rose. Before I know it, she's poured the water over the teabags and is looking for a spoon. I'm just about to rise to the bait when in bursts Seth Roberts singing some football chant from a five a side social they'd all been at on Sunday. They all fall about laughing as you can imagine. I look over to see Vanessa squashing the teabags against the side of the mugs and spooning them into the bin. All except mine that is. She hands the others out and then turns to me and says, and this is without eye contact, 'yours is on the side, I don't know how you have it'.

**Julia**   I see.

**Simon**   Which for the record is entirely untrue because I laminated a list of staff tea and coffee requirements and stuck it on the mug cupboard last week.

*Julia sits.*

**Julia**   I need five minutes.

**Simon**   Then Seth Roberts pipes up, 'Weak Vanessa, Jeeves likes it weak and watery.'
Are you alright Julia, you look wiped out.

**Julia**   I'm wiped out. I feel completely done in.

**Simon**   Have five minutes. A cup of tea?

**Julia**   I'm having five minutes.

*Takes off her shoes.*

**Simon**   You come to bed late.

**Julia**   I could be going down with something.

**Simon**   You never used to come to bed late.

**Julia**   I may have a virus.

**Simon**   Yesterday, you were in the bedroom getting dressed. The door was closed. I nearly knocked.

**Julia** *looks past* **Simon** *startled. Stands.*

**Simon**   And I thought ten years we've been together ten years and I felt I should knock. I stopped myself.

**Julia** *walks to the kitchen top.*

*Frantically looks for something.*

*Lifts things, looks to the floor.*

**Julia**   It's gone. I put it down.
I put it here.
Right here.

**Simon**   What?

**Julia**   My watch. I thought, I'll put it there. I'll leave it there and then I'll know.
Did you move it?

**Simon**   Your watch?

**Julia**   Yes, my bloody watch. Did you move it?

**Simon**   No. I haven't seen your watch.

**Julia**   It was there. That's where I put it. I put it there. Please
Simon.
Is this you?
Are you moving things?

**Simon**   Am I what? Moving things? What things?

**Julia**   Please, if it is you, please?

**Simon**   I don't know what you're talking about?

**Julia**   Something's not – there's something … Things are moving.

**Simon**   Moving?

**Julia**   I think someone's moving my things.

**Simon**   What?

**Julia**   Things are moving. Things. I put things down and then
they're not there.

*Pause.*

**Simon**   I don't understand.

**Julia**   My things. Some things have gone.

**Simon**   Gone!

**Julia**   I think.
I have a feeling.
I have a feeling that someone … and I know it sounds mental but
… It feels like someone is here. With us.
I can't shake the feeling that someone is here. I don't know.

**Simon**   There's no one here. You're being …

**Julia**   My things?

**Simon**   Right.

*Pause. Thinks.*

**Simon**   What things exactly?

**Julia** My perfume. The one I got with that voucher from your sister.
And some of my pants.

**Simon** Your pants?

**Julia** My knickers.

**Simon** Jesus Christ.

**Julia** I don't know. I thought it was me. But then the window.

**Simon** The window?

**Julia** Last night. I closed it and I know it's a bit dodgy but that's how I know I closed it. Because it's the one I check.
And last night I checked it and then when we get back it's open?

**Simon** Thing is.
Its all fine and this is fine to tell me but fucking hell
I'm like this (holds out his shaking hand to demonstrate flat line) and that's when I'm good. At the moment, at this point in my life – good is nothing.
Good is getting up, scratching my balls, getting dressed, going to work and absolutely nothing happening.
That is a good day.
So things moving and knickers and open windows and shit (shakes his flat-lining hand building to over-exaggerated shaking).

**Julia** I know this, (demonstrates the shaking hand) but that window can't just open, can it.

**Simon** 'Gone' you said?

**Julia** Not expensive stuff. It seems more sinister, not just stealing things but then also moving them.
Moving my things.
It's weird.

**Simon** '*Your* things' you said.

**Julia** I did, yes.

**Simon** Just things you put down and then they're not there?

**Julia**  Yes, sort of, I think.

**Simon**  You're so busy.
That's what it'll be. You're tired. Forgetting where you put things.

**Julia**  I thought that. I did.
I thought 'Oh, it's me, I'm knackered. Dementia starting.'
That's what I thought.
Then the window.

**Simon**  It must have been open.
I think I remember it being open. I'm sure – almost certain – I looked up at it and thought 'Oh the window's open, shit.'

**Julia**  I put my watch there.
I put it there.
I did. I'm certain.

*She sits back down.*

**Simon**  You look exhausted.

**Julia**  I'm tired.
I don't seem to be able to switch off.

**Simon**  You're never in bed before one.

**Julia**  My head is spinning with it all. The last few months.

**Simon**  You're up at six.

**Julia**  I don't think I'll ever get back up.

**Simon**  You should come to bed the same time as me.

**Julia**  Over and over in my head.

**Simon**  Please Julia.

**Julia**  I can't shake it.

**Simon**  Please.

**Julia**  I'm sorry. I'm tired.

**Simon**    Unsubstantiated. Insubstantial evidence. No basis for further investigation. Jesus Christ. These things happen all the time to teachers.

**Julia**    It was poetry slam tonight. Attendance was low.
Actually no one came.
Sue McGillis took it upon herself to volunteer two lads she had in detention.
The potential for disaster was great.
In they come with attitude and intimidation. A fight broke out almost immediately.
Sue took Kai Riches off to the staff room with her and I was left with Tyler Banks.

**Simon**    Right.

**Julia**    Divide and conquer.
He worked. Quietly. For almost half an hour. He curled his arm around his book. Chewed his top lip.
Like a child.

**Simon**    You made progress. That's good.

**Julia**    I asked him to read out his work.

'Girl you know I like it when you climb on top
Love muscles feel tighter than a headlock
And you know I love the way you make the bed rock
Take me to ecstasy without taking Ecstacy.'

It's a rap. 50 cents. He was aggressive and frowning.

**Simon**    Right.

**Julia**    I told him it was good. That I liked it. That he should feel free to express himself in any way he wanted.

**Simon**    Yes.

**Julia**    His face softened. I saw it. He softened. With flattery. It took me by surprise.
He was looking for approval. Like a child.

**Simon**    Julia.

**Julia**  He looked at my tits.

I let him. I caught his eye. He licked his lips.

I noticed he has quite a substantial amount of bristles on his chin.
And a broad back. His hands are unexpectedly large I thought. But
he is six foot. So.

I looked at his crotch.

**Simon**    I don't know what you're trying to do.

**Julia**    Although he is only fifteen I thought how absurd it would
be to imagine that he was an innocent. He possessed some sort of
instinct I thought for this sort of sexual play and then I thought
that it was quite delicious actually his instinctive raw unashamed
hunger. He looked like he wanted to gobble me up.

**Simon**    Please, stop it.

**Julia**    I waited for a twinge. A feeling. Something. Excitement.
But there was nothing. Actually not nothing. I felt shifty.
Unsettled. I thought of his face softening. Of his searching
approval. And even though he looked at me with a convincing
level of sexual want. I saw that he is a child.

**Simon**    What do you want me to say?

**Julia**    At the time there was talk of a book. A diary. A diary. With
details of a seemingly inappropriate relationship. The diary that
was given to the Head.

**Simon**    A book of lies.

**Julia**    What happened to the diary?

**Simon**    I don't know.

**Julia**    It's that one thing. Because without it there's nothing, no
case. But it's in here. *(head)*

**Simon**    He said. The head said it was nothing more than fantasy.
A teenage fantasy.

**Julia**    Where is it?

**Simon**    Forget about the diary. The diary is gone.

*A dim pool of light isolates a solitary Victorian sash window.*

*A shadow behind the glass. Hands pulling at the window. Struggling. Pulling. Heaving. Eventually it gives and opens.*

*Steph climbs through.*

*She stands lit by moonlight in front of the window. In a bedroom. She stands. A long time. She breathes in. Smells the air.*

**Julia**  I saw her.
I. Saw. Her.

**Simon**  You've seen her?

**Julia**  I looked for her. I went to where she lives.
I had a feeling. A gut feeling when I saw her.

**Simon**  Then you've seen the sort of kid she is. Where she's from. The mother. Did you see the mother?

**Julia**  I saw truth. I felt it. I saw truth in her.

*She moves. Towards a traditional large pine dressing table, centre stage. (The dressing table has a large oval mirror in the centre with the glass out so the effect is a see through mirror).*

*She touches things.*

**Simon**  I think it's all got too much, I think you need to rest. To sleep. You'll feel better after a good night's sleep.

**Julia**  The diary was in your drawer.

**Simon**  No.

**Julia**  In the dresser.

*Fingers designer scarves and necklaces that are draped around the mirror. Runs her hand over expensive pots and creams and polishes and sprays. She sprays the air. Sniffs. Rubs her nose. Throws the perfume. She opens the pots and creams, sniffs them.*

**Simon**  There was no diary.

**Julia**  And now it's gone.

**Simon**    It wasn't there.

**Julia**    I saw a book.

*Picks up lipsticks and brushes. Plays with them, applies them crudely, childlike.*

**Simon**    You've been through my things.

**Julia**    My ring has gone.

*Opens the drawers, takes out tampons, letters, bits and bobs. Opens another drawer, takes out expensive lingerie, pretty bras and lacy knickers. Examines them, fingers the pretty soft fabrics, smells them, closes her eyes, breathes them in.*

**Simon**    Your wedding ring?

**Julia**    I thought it might have dropped into your drawer.

**Simon**    Your wedding ring?

**Julia**    My ring wasn't there.
I saw the book had gone.

**Simon**    You read it.

**Julia**    I thought – I need to believe you – I wanted to trust you.

**Simon**    You *wanted* to? You *wanted* to trust me?

**Julia**    I trust you.

**Simon**    But you went back.

**Julia**    I saw a book and now it's gone.

**Simon**    You looked for it?

**Julia**    Yes.

*Steph opens her eyes and sees herself in the mirror. Looks at herself.*

**Simon** *leaves.*

*Julia stands.*

*Paces.*

*Confused.*

*Distressed.*

*Picks up her bag and leaves.*

*Steph picks up nail scissors and looks at the knickers – thinks about it.*

*Looks at herself.*

*Puts the scissors down. The lingerie away. Closes the drawers.*

*Looks at herself.*

*Rubs at her face. Pulling her face. Lifts her hair pulling it this way and that, drags it down. Flattens it with her sticky palms. Flatter and flatter. Finds a band and ties it back as flat as it will go. She finds wipes and cleans off her face. Rubbing it clean, rubbing it free.*

*Looks at herself.*

*Again picks up the scissors. Picks up her hair. Starts to cut off her hair. Timidly at first then builds to great chunks. So finally she is left with short cropped hair.*

*She looks at herself. Ignores the hair all around her.*

*\*Her own reflection catches and holds her.*

*Unrecognisable.*

*Indifferent.*

*A long time.*

*As long as she can comfortably get away with as the light fades to darkness.*

*\****Melissa*** *is in the kitchen.*

*Her hair's in velcro rollers.*

*She checks herself out in a hand-held mirror.*

*She's got a big bag of makeup on the table.*

*She's peeling veg into a bowl.*

**Steph** *enters.*

*Home from school.*

*She has a beanie on.*

*She is caked in mud. Her hands, her face.*

*Obviously had her hands in earth.*

*She holds poppies in her hands, with earth attached. Recently dug.*

**Melissa** *carries on peeling veg doesn't look at* **Steph**.

**Steph**   What you doing?

**Melissa**   You're home early?

**Steph**   Finished early.

**Steph** *puts the poppies on the side.*

**Melissa**   Whatever, Steph.

**Steph**   What you doing?

**Melissa**   What?

**Steph**   This. What's this? There's a table cloth? And is that
– mats?

**Melissa**   What? Yeah.

**Steph**   Yeah.
Is this for me? Cloths and mats?
Makes me nervous.

**Melissa**   Right.

*Looks at* **Steph** *for first time.*

**Melissa**   What's that? Mud? Is that mud. What have you … Have
you been digging?

**Steph**   Saw some flowers.

**Melissa**   You're covered in mud?

**Steph**   I am, yes. I'll have a bath.

**Melissa**   I give up.

**Steph**   I feel like a bath.

**Melissa**   Right. You do that.

**Steph**   Is this for me?

**Melissa**   What?

**Steph**   This – candles?

*(Beat)*

Not for me.

**Melissa**   No.

**Steph**   Right. So you're having someone over. For tea? Janine?

*(Beat)*

No. Who then?

**Melissa**   That fella. The one from before.

**Steph**   The soldier? He came back?

**Melissa**   He did.

**Steph**   That's something then.

*Takes off her hat, revealing her hair.*

**Melissa**   Your hair?

**Steph**   What is he? Your boyfriend? Is that what he is?

**Melissa**   What have you done?

**Steph**   How many times do you fuck someone before they're your boyfriend?

**Melissa**   What have you done to your hair, Steph?

**Steph**  Or are you just 'seeing' him.
Is he just a 'friend'.
Too old for uncles! That's one thing.

**Melissa**  Stephanie.
What have you done to your hair?

**Steph**  Oh yeah, that. Fancied a change.
You know me, always messing with my hair.
Ever happy.

**Melissa**  Something's happened?

**Steph**  Nothing's happened.

**Melissa**  You changed your hair.

**Steph**  What of it.

**Melissa**  This hair's about something.

*Stop.*

*Look at each other.*

**Steph**  I'm getting in the way. Don't let me stop you. You carry on.

**Melissa**  You're gonna tell me about this hair.

**Steph**  I'm a teenager you know what we're like.

**Melissa**  No. This – this isn't you.

**Steph**  It's my hair. My hair. I cut it.

**Melissa**  *You. You* cut your hair. Where?

**Steph**  Where?

**Melissa**  Yes, where?

**Steph**  What does it matter, where?

**Melissa**  You go to school and you comes back with your hair like that?

**Steph**  I done it last night, actually. Not that you'd know.

**Melissa**   You're not wearing makeup.

**Steph**   That's a crime is it.

**Melissa**   You're dressing like a boy.

**Steph**   I don't believe you.

**Melissa**   Now the hair … It's not you.

**Steph**   This is me.

**Melissa**   I don't see you.

**Steph**   You don't look.

**Steph** *storms off.*

**Melissa** *carries on making up.*

*\*Fusses her hair.*

*After a while goes to the poppies.*

*Light fades to black.*

*A modern family kitchen.*

*Lunchtime. Weekday.*

*\*Julia dressed and stressed. Coat on, bag on shoulder.*

*Simon unkempt.*

*Not dressed.*

**Simon**   There was dust. It's started. That's what I thought.

**Julia**   Right.

**Simon**   I'd run the shower. I was going to dress. I could feel it. 'Today', I thought 'I'm going to dress'.

**Julia**   And then.

**Simon**   And then there was no soap. So I came down to the kitchen to get some soap from under the sink.

**Julia**   Not the bathroom cabinet?

**Simon**   There was none in the cabinet Julia. It made sense to try under the sink. And then it happened.

**Julia**   Dust you said.

**Simon**   Practically rubble.

**Julia**   Practically.

**Simon**   The next stage would have been rubble.

**Julia**   It looks fine.

**Simon**   Now. It looks fine now. There was shaking. I swear there was shaking.

**Julia**   Right.

**Simon**   We should never have got your father in. We should have got someone who can bend and see.

**Julia**   He likes to help.

**Simon**   The whole sodding house is going to fall down.

**Julia**   No. It's not.

**Simon**   The ceiling will cave in and it'll be just my sodding luck to be stood underneath it looking for soap in a place where the bloody soap shouldn't have been to start with.
Naked. I'll probably be naked.

**Julia**   You called me at work.

**Simon**   I'd be in the local papers. Seth Roberts would love that. He'd love it alright. It'd be all about dropping your soap, watching your cracks and all that locker room stuff.

**Julia**   You called me at work. For this.

**Simon**   He'd not let it drop.

**Julia**   I have to go. To work.

**Simon**   You have to? Is there any point? I don't know that there's any point?

**Julia**    I work. I should be at work and I'm here. With you.
Listening to you.

**Simon**    By the time you get there it will be time to come home.

**Julia**    I have poetry slam.

**Simon**    Cancel it.

**Julia**    No.

**Simon**    I'll cook. I'll make something nice. Something without carbs.

**Julia**    I won't want anything.

**Steph** *enters kitchen.*

**Melissa** *plays with the poppy on the table.*

**Simon**    Vegetables. Chicken.

**Julia**    For Christ sake.
I should get back. I need to work. Can't have both of us, sick.

**Simon**    I'm not sick.

**Melissa**    Peace offering?

**Steph** *says nothing.*

**Melissa**    You know why the poppy is a symbol of remembrance?

*Nothing.*

**Melissa**    Poppies were the first flowers to grow in the earth on the soldiers' graves in France.
Imagine that, Steph.
Poppies, in all that sad brown earth. There's a poem.

**Steph**    In Flanders fields.

**Melissa**    In Flanders fields. I remembers that from school. All them graves. Them soldiers.
The churned up earth with all them men, underneath.
The lives they could have had.

**Steph**    And then there's just a field, a churned up field. But in time out of the earth comes the most perfect piece of nature and life.

**Melissa**    That's some sight, I reckon.
A field of poppies.

**Steph**    Yeah. Reckon it is.

**Steph**    Them poppies aren't a symbol of remembrance, Mam. You know what I thinks of when I thinks of them poppies?

**Melissa**    What?

**Steph**    Resurrection.

**Simon**    It's just with the break in. Last night.

**Julia**    You should get dressed, at least.

**Simon**    He was very understanding I thought. When I phoned him earlier. The head. Said at least it wasn't shit. Said he'd heard of people having shit up the walls with a break in. Said head of Maths in his previous school had come home to 'cunt' spelt out in shit over the walls. I think that would be worse. So. It was just a shock. An invasion. Someone in your home.

**Julia**    A violation.

*Drops her bag.*

*Steph and Melissa in kitchen.*

*Melissa is sat at the table, peeling potatoes into a washing up bowl.*

**Melissa**    I'll phone him. Tell him not to come. We'll have a night in, shall we. A girls' night.
Just you and me.

**Steph**    If you want.

**Melissa**    I want.
You know, it used to be amazing yer.
Won awards theses flats did. When they was first built.

Used to be a good area.

**Steph**    People like you moved in.
Area goes downhill fast with people like you in it.

**Melissa**    Cheeky sod you are.

*Look at each other and laugh.*

Nice to have you smiling.

*Pause.*

What's that thing.
You know that thing when good goes to good and bad to bad and
all that.

**Steph**    Karma.
Eye for an eye.
Two wrongs make a right.

**Melissa**    Two wrongs don't make a right. That's the saying.

**Steph**    I know the saying.

**Melissa**    You said it wrong. It's a proverb. There, that's
something else I learned in school.
A proverb.

**Steph**    I knows that. I knows what I said.

**Melissa**    You said it wrong.

**Steph**    Two wrongs make a right. Like evens init.
So. You scratch my car with a key. I kick in your fence. Two
wrongs. Now it's fair. Everything's evens.

**Melissa**    Two wrongs makes a right it is.
Come on, get your hands dirty. I'm gonna do us the best cooked
dinner ever.

*Passes her a veg knife.*

**Steph**    Christ does the oven work, does it?

**Melissa**    You got a nerve you.

*(beat)*
I dunno. You better check. The hob works. I'll do a stew.
Bung it all in.

**Steph**    Sounds divine.

**Simon**    What's the matter?

**Julia**    What's the matter?
Somebody broke into our home.
Sat in our bedroom and cut off their hair. Not somebody.
Her.
It was her, wasn't it?

**Simon**    You don't know that. We don't know.

**Julia**    She broke into our home.
And I want to know why.

*A look.*

*Hold the look as long as they can.*

**Simon** *breaks the look.*

*Paces.*

**Julia** *leaves the kitchen.*

**Simon** *pacing.*

*Paces.*

*Doesn't know what to do with himself.*

*Melissa flicks water at Steph. Steph flicks back.*

*Laughs.*

**Melissa**    There you go. Two wrongs makes a right!
I flick you, you flicks me.
Now we're square.

**Steph**    You know them people, them in the big houses I was
telling you about. They'd say that one that you said. Two wrongs
don't make a right. They'd say that cos they thinks it makes them

look good. Like they're all forgiving an' that. They lives in a
world where they pretends to be something they're not.
There's no peace in their lives, Mam.
Cos they eats away at you lies. They eats away at you till you
can't see straight no more.
I believe that Mam.
I believe that one hundred per cent cos I seen it.

**Simon** *sweeps the contents of the table to the floor.*

**Melissa**    Are you gonna be any help to me? You can get started
on them carrots.

**Steph**    He'll get it worse living the lie.
I think he's a kind man. I do. I think he is kind. Sometimes.
Which sometimes makes me feel bad but there you go.
Am I pretty?

**Melissa**    What?

**Steph**    Me.
Am I pretty do you think?

**Melissa**    Are you pretty?
I suppose.

**Steph**    I am.
I am pretty.
I know that.

**Melissa**    Good. Good for you.

**Steph**    I have something.
That thing.
Something about me.

**Melissa**    I don't know.

**Steph**    I do. I see it.
I don't know what it is.
They sees it. Men.

**Melissa**    Stop it.

**Steph**    They sees it. He saw it.

**Melissa**    Stop it.

**Steph**    I thought he liked me.

**Melissa**    Yeah.

**Steph**    I trusted him. I thought he was kind.

**Melissa**    You know, I worked in the Lion after I had you.

**Steph**    No, I didn't know.

**Melissa**    Cos I was skint.

**Steph**    You're always skint.

**Melissa**    You was about one.
I didn't want to leave you. But.
Didn't have a choice.
My Dad died.
Didn't have no one else. No one to turn to.
There was this woman, Tanya, lived in the flat next door and she
took you in so I could go out an
earn a couple of bob. You was no bother.
You was gorgeous. Big brown eyes, only had eyes for me.
You never cried.
Then I got a couple of days work down the road in the post office.
I thought my shit was chocolate with that little job. I did. I thought
it was.
Cos it was a step up, you know, from the pub.
I hated that pub, stinking of booze and fags and all the men, pissed
up trying to cop a feel.
But them couple of days in the post office. I thought that was
proper, it was respectable. Like an office job sort of thing.
*(beat)*
After a while the boss, he said I'd been nicking from him.
Said he was gonna call it in. Tell the police.
I had though, that was the thing.
I was beside myself. Cos it was bad enough that I was on my
own but then I thought if I ends up banged up and they takes you

off me. I thought that would be it, like. That would be the end for me.
Then he says he can sort it out for me.
He knows a way I can pay him back.
I didn't know what else to do.
I didn't like it but I could blank it out, in my head, pretend it weren't happening.
But then he keeps coming at me.
Coming back for more.
So, I tells him 'no'.
One day, I just comes out with it. 'No'.
He knocked the shit outta me.

*Pause.*

**Steph**   Mam.

**Julia** *comes back to the kitchen.*

**Julia**   What's that?

**Simon** *looks to where* **Julia** *is pointing.*

**Julia**   Under your papers. What is it?

**Simon**   What?
I don't know.

**Julia**   What do you mean you don't know?

**Simon**   I don't know. I don't know what you're looking at.

**Julia**   I'm looking under your papers. There. Sticking out.

**Simon**   I don't know.

**Julia**   Under your papers, for Christ sake.

**Simon**   It's nothing. It's nothing Julia.

**Julia**   You don't know. You said you don't know.

**Simon**   No. I've never seen it before.

**Julia**   How do you know its nothing then?

**Simon**   I know.

**Julia**   It looks like a book.

**Simon**   Please, it's nothing.

**Simon** *covers it. Hides it.*

**Julia**   It's the diary. Is it the diary?

**Simon**   I don't know how it got there. I don't.

**Julia**   I want to see it.

**Julia** *moves to get it.* **Simon** *stops her.*

**Simon**   It will upset you.

**Julia**   Why will it upset me?

**Simon**   He gave it to me. The head. He said it was a work of
fiction. Didn't want it getting in the wrong hands. The cleaners,
you know, they go through everything and his secretary.
He said. He said to put it somewhere.

**Julia**   But it was evidence.

**Simon**   I had it. And I didn't know what to do.
Believe me, Julia. I didn't know what to do with it.

**Julia**   You shouldn't have taken it.

**Simon**   I kept it. And then I thought the house might be searched.
I don't know. I'm not a criminal. This is all new to me. I don't
know how these things work. I thought it could be used against
me in some way so I hid it.

**Julia**   I think if the police were going to search this house for
indecent material I think one of the first places they'd look is your
drawer in the dressing table.

**Simon**   I hid it under the floorboards. In the bathroom. But then
what with the leak and your father.
I moved it.

**Julia**   To your drawer.

**Simon**   And then it went.
It went missing. I didn't move it again. It just went.
I thought it was you.

**Julia**   Me?

**Simon**   And I haven't seen it since. Until now. Until there.

**Julia**   Give it to me.

**Simon**   No. It's just a diary.

**Julia**   Her diary.

**Simon**   I'll burn it. It'll be gone. By the time you come home.
It'll be gone.

**Julia**   You kept it. You kept it, Simon.

**Simon**   Yes.

**Julia**   Why did you keep it?
Jesus Christ, why did you keep it?
Because you'd destroy it. Normal people would destroy it.
I would have destroyed it.
But you kept it. Hid it. Protected it.
Why?

**Simon**   I don't know.

**Julia**   Give it to me.

**Simon**   A teenager's ramblings. A stupid teenager rambling.

**Julia**   Give me the fucking diary.

**Simon**   No. Please Julia.

**Julia** *launches at him, hits him. He takes hold of her hands to stop her.*

**Julia**   Please. Please for fuck's sake, Simon.

*Simon surrenders the fight.*

*Gives Julia the diary.*

*An exercise book with scribbling on the covers.*

**Simon**    It's a situation. A situation and there are two sides. There are most definitely two sides to this. There are illusions. And impressions. It is a book of illusions and impressions.

*Pacing. Anxious.*

*She sits and opens it.*

*Reads.*

**Simon**    The newspapers. The hacking. The journalists you know. They thought it was okay. How within their profession it was an accepted practice. It was almost ridiculous that we would not have realised. Because that happens I think. The way your behaviour in the safety of your own world becomes common practice or simply perfectly acceptable.
It's only when you step out of this you realise it's not right at all.
But historically this happens Julia. The MP's expenses, corrupt police, soldiers and that water blasting and torture. That sort of thing.
Perfectly normal people in an abnormal world, even the holocaust.
We judge them but we have not stood in their shoes.
Don't tell me they all were evil. All of them.
Everyone who knew what was going on.
All the soldiers, their wives, families, cleaners, cooks.
Even people who lived nearby. It was a practice
that was acceptable in their world.
In their wartime.

*He is still pacing and anxious.*

**Julia** *looks up from the diary.*

**Julia**    There are letters.
It says here there are letters.

**Simon**    She says a lot of things that aren't true.

**Julia**    She wrote you letters.

**Simon**    Not true. Not me.

**Julia**   Where are the letters?

**Simon**   No letters.
No letters Julia.

*Julia puts the book down.*

**Julia**   You're lying. You are lying to me.

*Gets up.*

*Gets herself a glass of water.*

**Simon**   No.
There was no case. Nothing to answer to. Unsubstantiated.
For Christ sake.

*Stands and looks out of the kitchen window into the garden.*

**Simon**   Are you not happy. Will you not be happy until I'm
rocking in a straitjacket in a cell. Is that what you want? Do you
want me repeatedly banging my head and dribbling in some cell
somewhere.

*Still looking out of the window.*

**Julia**   The poppies are dead Simon.
They didn't come to anything. Which is a shame I think because
the promise of them was really quite splendid.
The weight and length of their stem has made them curl over.
They've unearthed. Their roots are exposed.
I can see the soil around them. There's something else.
Underneath the soil something just showing.
It looks like a case of some sort. I think it may well be the
briefcase you lost. The one I bought you when you were made
Head of department.

Are the letters in the briefcase Simon?

**Simon**   I was kind to her. I should have known better. It was
Seth. Seth Roberts. You know how he was. How he is. How he
made me feel. He bullied me Julia. Bullied me for years. And he
was saying all this stuff and I didn't stop it. I didn't stop him. I
watched. I watched him. And I said nothing. I did nothing.

*Julia goes to the door, exits.*

**Steph**    I was waiting for him, I wanted to show him this thing I'd seen cos he was helping me, talking about my future.

Talking about me having a career an all that. He thought if I worked hard I'd be able to go to college even get a degree if I wanted. And I waited for him but he didn't come and then so I went down to the staff room to look out for him and there's no one around. Even the cleaners have gone by now. I can see the back of him.

Then I heard him talking to this other teacher and they was taking the piss. This one, Mr Roberts.

Seth Roberts they calls him, I think you knows him, he likes the dark.

He's saying that I'm some sort of easy pussy. Saying that he needed to watch himself around me.

My sort.

Saying that not so long ago a girl of my age would've been fair game. Legal. Said it's since women got the vote and contraception. Said that was when we stopped knowing our place. That was when all the trouble started. And he was laughing. And I was thinking you wait Simon's gonna give it to you both barrels now mate. He won't have you getting away with that. But you know what. He stood there laughing with him. Laughing at me. At me, mum.

I couldn't breathe. I thought my throat was closing. And my eyes was watering. It weren't crying. It was like I'd steamed up. Boiled over. I went out into the lane behind the carpark and I thought I'd scratch all their cars you know so I could breathe again. And he's coming after me.

**Melissa**    Simon had seen you?

**Steph**    Not Simon. No. Not Simon, Mam. Seth. He came after me.

Seth is in the lane. And he's looking at me. Looking through me. Looking through my clothes at my

tits, looking down me. I try to run past him. But he's grabbed me before I can get anywhere and he's putting his hand up my skirt. I

can feel his cock pushing through them stupid trousers they wear.
And I know what's going to happen, Mam. I knows all about that
don't I.
But I can't do nothing.
He's grabbing at my tits and then I sees he's got his cock in his
hand.
And he's forcing my head down. Forcing it in my mouth.
And its making me gag but he's pushing it harder in. And then I
looks up and I sees him.
At the top of the lane. Simon.
I can see him. And he's just stood there. He's not doing nothing.
He's not helping me. He's watching. Just stood there watching.
And then he lets go of me. Puts himself away, does himself up like
he's just finished a piss or something normal like.
And he goes back to Simon and he laughs about something,
smacks Simon on the back and they walks off back to school.
He looked back.
Simon.

**Simon** *talks after her – carries on, when she is off stage.*

**Simon**    Truth?
You said you saw truth in her. The irony.
She has a foul mouth. Her mother's a whore. You didn't know that
did you? A prostitute. Has a regular patch down the viaduct. She's
been giving Seth blow jobs for the last four years. This is who
we're talking about Julia. These people.

**Julia** *re-enters with the briefcase covered in mud.*

**Simon**    And you'd believe them.
You'd believe her.
Over someone like me.

*She throws the briefcase, hits him, screams at him, loses it.*

*Then composes herself and leaves the room.*

**Simon** *is left on stage with the briefcase.*

**Steph**    I knew he wouldn't do nothing.
Wouldn't say what had happened.

Wouldn't stand up for me. I saw that in him.
At that moment. And that got to me more than the other stuff,
Mam. He let me down.
That made me feel like nothing.
That was a wrong.

**Melissa**    Yes. That was a wrong.

**Steph**    They would have come here, you know that don't you.
They would have looked at us. At you.
They wouldn't have done nothing.
Evil prevails when a good man does nothing.

*Blackout.*

**End**